POLAR BEAR VS. ORCA

Lisa M. Bolt Simons

CAPSTONE PRESS
a capstone imprint

Published by Capstone Press, an imprint of Capstone
1710 Roe Crest Drive, North Mankato, Minnesota 56003
capstonepub.com

Library of Congress Cataloging-in-Publication Data
Names: Simons, Lisa M. B., 1969– author.
Title: Polar bear vs. orca / by Lisa M. Bolt Simons.
Description: North Mankato, Minnesota : Capstone Press, [2022] | Series: Predator
  vs. predator | Includes bibliographical references and index. | Audience: Ages
  8–11 | Audience: Grades 4–6
Identifiers: LCCN 2021012636 (print) | LCCN 2021012637 (ebook) | ISBN
  9781663914095 (hardcover) | ISBN 9781663914170 (pdf) | ISBN 9781663914194
  (kindle edition)
Subjects: LCSH: Polar bear—Juvenile literature. | Killer whale—Juvenile literature.
Classification: LCC QL737.C27 S558 2022 (print) | LCC QL737.C27 (ebook) |
  DDC 599.786—dc23
LC record available at https://lccn.loc.gov/2021012636
LC ebook record available at https://lccn.loc.gov/2021012637

Summary: The icy cold Arctic is home to two mighty predators—the powerful polar bear and intelligent orca. But which animal is the fiercest of the ecosystem? Does the polar bear's patience in stalking its prey and strength in attack put it on top? Or does the orca's ability to work in a pod give it the edge? Compare and contrast each animal's features and skills before you declare the winning predator.

Image Credits
Getty Images: Foto4440, bottom 19; Minden Pictures: Doug Allan/NPL, 13, Hiroya Minakuchi, top 19; Newscom: Eme/ZUMA Press, 27; Shutterstock: Andrey_Kuzmin, (scratches) design element, Bonma Suriya, (scratch) design element, buchpetzer, 5, Edwin Butter, left Cover, top 6, top 10, top 14, top 18, top 22, GTW, bottom 11, top left 28, HaseHoch2, (lightning) design element, hideto999, (water) design element, jo Crebbin, 21, JonathanJonesCreate, 23, Mario_Hoppmann, top 11, Nagel Photography, 9, Nina B, top right 28, Nora Yusuf, 15, ReVelStockArt, (font) design element, Risto Raunio, 4, Samantha Crimmin, 20, SergeyBitos, (frames) design element, SerGRAY, (screen) design element, slowmotiongli, middle Cover, middle 6, middle 10, middle 14, middle 18, middle 22, Stephen Lew, 12, Sylvie Bouchard, 8, Tory Kallman, 7, 17, vladsilver, 25

Editorial Credits
Editors: Gena Chester and Aaron Sautter; Designer: Elyse White; Media Researcher: Kelly Garvin; Production Specialist: Laura Manthe

TABLE OF CONTENTS

INTRO
Predators of the Arctic..........4

CHAPTER 1
Fast Forward........................6

CHAPTER 2
Super Strength 10

CHAPTER 3
Excellent Endurance 14

CHAPTER 4
Sneaky Strikes 18

CHAPTER 5
Unique Arctic Abilities 22

GLOSSARY 30
READ MORE 31
INTERNET SITES..............31
INDEX 32

Words in **bold** are in the glossary.

Predators of the Arctic

You may know the Arctic **biome** is cold. But did you know it's not made of solid land? This unique area is actually made of moving ice sheets. The seasons also set the Arctic apart. In the winter, most days have no sunlight. In the summer, the sun does not set on many days.

Predators, such as the polar bear and the orca, do well in the Arctic. Their **adaptations** help them survive. A polar bear uses its huge paws to walk on ice. An orca's body has blubber, a type of fat, that helps it survive in frigid water.

A polar bear runs across sea ice.

An orca swims in the Arctic Ocean.

Polar bears and orcas are predators. They eat other animals, or prey. Predators use speed, strength, and technique to hunt prey. Predators and prey **evolve** to survive. This evolution balances their **ecosystem.**

Frozen Deserts

Parts of the Arctic are actually called deserts because they're so dry. Arctic temperatures may drop as low as minus 40 degrees Fahrenheit (minus 40 degrees Celsius). Northern parts of Europe, Russia, Alaska, and Canada, as well as the Arctic Ocean, Greenland, and small islands, are all part of the Arctic. Polar bears only live in the Arctic. Orcas live in the Arctic, but they also live in other oceans around the world.

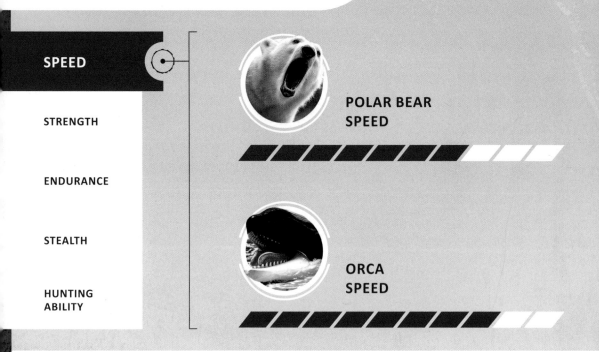

SPEED

STRENGTH

ENDURANCE

STEALTH

HUNTING ABILITY

POLAR BEAR SPEED

ORCA SPEED

Polar bears and orcas are fast swimmers. They need to be fast to catch prey.

One of the orca's fastest prey is the sea lion. It can reach speeds up to 25 miles (40 kilometers) per hour. But the orca can catch up. It can reach speeds up to 34 miles (54 km) per hour.

The octopus is another prey of the orca. Unless the octopus ducks into a tight space to hide, it's no match for the speedy orca.

Orcas usually swim at an average speed of 8 miles (13 km) per hour.

FACT

An orca is also called a killer whale. But it's not a whale. It's actually the largest member of the dolphin family.

Polar bears are expert swimmers.

As a marine mammal, the polar bear is also a fast swimmer. It swims up to 6 miles (10 km) per hour. Its slightly webbed front paws act like paddles. Its back paws steer.

One of the polar bear's prey is the seal. Typically, a seal matches a polar bear's speed at about 6 miles (10 km) per hour. But some seals can swim as fast as 18 miles (29 km) per hour to escape a predator. The polar bear's attack must be quick.

The polar bear is also speedy on land. It has small, soft bumps on its paws and sharp claws to help it grip the ice. Fur between its toes stops it from slipping. The polar bear can run up to 25 miles (40 km) per hour when hunting.

Cool Adaptations

The polar bear has many cool adaptations to survive the Arctic. It has 12-inch- (30-centimeter-) wide paws that walk easily over ice and snow. It also has three eyelids to protect its eyes from the cold and wind. Its body is covered in 4 inches (10 cm) of fat and a double-layered fur coat. These give the Arctic animal extra warmth.

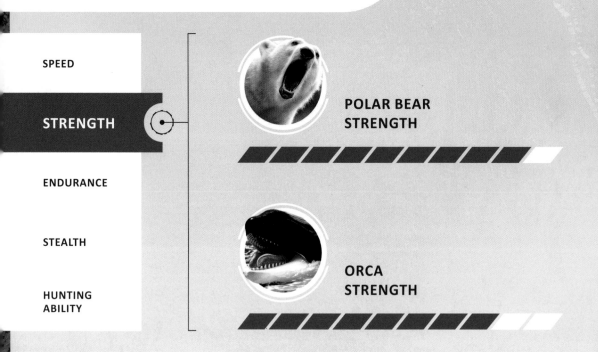

SPEED

STRENGTH

ENDURANCE

STEALTH

HUNTING
ABILITY

**POLAR BEAR
STRENGTH**

**ORCA
STRENGTH**

The polar bear is a strong Arctic predator.
Males can weigh up to 1,700 pounds (771 kg)
and can stand almost 10 feet (3 m) tall. In fact,
the polar bear is the biggest and strongest land
carnivore in the world.

FACT

Polar bear fur is not white—even though
it looks like it is. The hairs are see-through
and reflect the white snow.

A polar bear searches for its prey.

The polar bear hunts ringed seals and bearded seals the most. If the polar bear can't capture a seal on land, it might swim to catch its meal.

Once the polar bear kills its prey, it uses its strong bite to eat. This Arctic predator has sharp teeth. Its **canines** are larger than a grizzly bear's.

A polar bear captures a seal.

Like polar bears, orcas are strong. They hunt all kinds of animals from squid to sharks.

An orca can fit small prey such as penguins into its mouth. It strips off the skin and feathers and spits them out. Then the orca swallows the meat. An orca's sharp teeth tear and rip apart large prey.

Orcas also hunt penguins near Antarctica.

An orca pod wave washes a seal.

Orcas are smart too. Climate change has forced orcas to come up with new ways to hunt. One way is called wave washing. A group, or pod, of orcas swim just under the surface toward a seal atop a floating piece of ice. The orcas' motion creates a wave that knocks the seal off the ice. If the seal climbs back before the orcas can attack, the pod will wave wash it again.

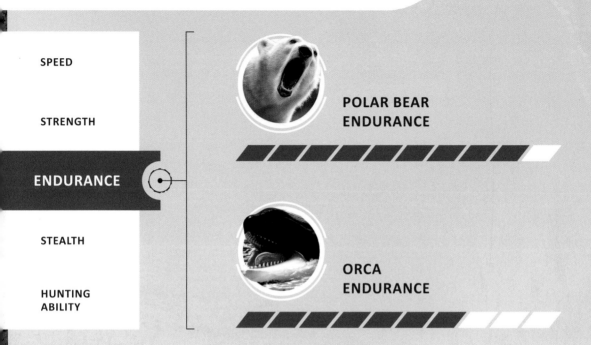

SPEED

STRENGTH

ENDURANCE

STEALTH

HUNTING ABILITY

POLAR BEAR ENDURANCE

ORCA ENDURANCE

A polar bear not only has strength, but it also has **endurance**. It can swim without resting for hours, even days, as it hunts. The polar bear's long, flexible neck allows it to come up often for air. It hunts walruses and other prey by swimming between ice pieces. In the open water, it hunts for fish.

The polar bear has a 2 to 4.5-inch (5 to 11.5-cm) layer of fat. This layer keeps the polar bear warm as it swims and hunts in cold water. Fat also floats. It helps keep the polar bear from sinking.

A polar bear swims between ice pieces in the Arctic Ocean.

The orca has excellent endurance too. It has an advantage over the polar bear. When a polar bear is tired, it doesn't have other polar bears to help with the hunt. The orca has a pod. The pod's combined endurance is greater than one animal.

When orcas wave wash prey like seals, the seals try to survive. If the seal is washed off the ice piece, it may jump back on top. But orcas do not give up easily. Wave washing can last for hours.

On its own, a single orca can swim long distances. It swims an average of 40 miles (64 km) a day.

Half Asleep

An orca sleeps with half of its brain at a time. One eye closes that is opposite to the side of the brain that sleeps. This is called unihemispheric sleep. By sleeping this way, orcas never lose full **consciousness** like humans do.

A pod of orcas

SPEED

STRENGTH

ENDURANCE

STEALTH

HUNTING
ABILITY

**POLAR BEAR
STEALTH**

**ORCA
STEALTH**

Polar bears and orcas are strong and quick hunters. They also use stealth to stalk their prey, which makes them successful Arctic predators.

Orcas work as a team to stalk their prey. Some orcas swim around until they find a school of fish. They blow bubbles to scare the fish. A small group of fish gets separated from the larger school. The orcas surround them. The orcas will slap the fish with their **flukes** until the fish are knocked out or killed.

A pod of orcas hunts fish.

Other pods of orcas split up from each other and use their numbers to surround prey. They cut off a seal's escape route this way. They take their time and close in on the seal for the kill.

Orcas wait near the shore for prey.

The polar bear is a stealthy predator. It uses its sense of smell to help stalk its prey. It can find prey more than 0.5 mile (1 km) away with its nose.

A polar bear is patient. It can smell breathing holes in the ice that seals use. A polar bear will wait at a hole for hours or days for the seal to pop up to breathe. Then it attacks.

A polar bear waits by a breathing hole used by seals.

Polar bears sometimes attack prey from the water.

A polar bear might also sneak up on a seal on floating ice. The predator swims downwind of the seal so that the seal won't smell it. Once the polar bear is behind the seal, it waits. Then the polar bear rises out of the water and pounces! If the seal escapes, the polar bear can dive into the water after it.

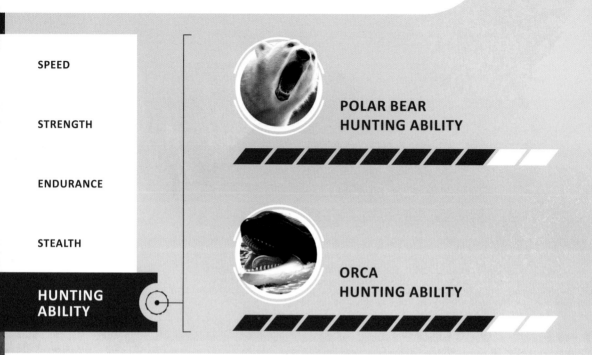

SPEED

STRENGTH

ENDURANCE

STEALTH

HUNTING
ABILITY

**POLAR BEAR
HUNTING ABILITY**

**ORCA
HUNTING ABILITY**

The polar bear and orca are predators with unique hunting abilities. Besides a polar bear's sensitive nose, it also has a good sense of hearing. It can hear seals swimming under the thick ice.

A polar bear can go a long time without food. The polar bear hunts a lot, but kills are rare. When it does manage to get food, the polar bear eats the fat of the animal first. This gives the polar bear enough energy to survive.

Polar bears use their strong senses of smell and hearing to hunt for prey.

FACT

The polar bear's scientific name, *Ursus Maritimus*, means "sea bear" in Latin.

Like the polar bear, the orca has an excellent sense of hearing. While the polar bear hears with its ears, the orca gets sound through its jawbone.

Orcas use **echolocation**, just like bats. They make sounds that pass through the water. The sound waves bounce off objects like fish. Then they return to the orca as an echo. Orcas find fish using this ability.

Orcas speak with each other in their pods when they hunt. First, one orca spyhops. This a move where half of the orca's body comes straight out of the water to look for prey. If the orca sees a walrus, then it tells the pod. But when they start hunting, they're silent. A surprise attack will catch more prey.

An orca spyhopping to spot its prey.

THE DANGER OF CLIMATE CHANGE

Climate change is affecting these Arctic predators. In 1980, there were over 2.96 billion square miles (7.67 billion square kilometers) of Arctic sea ice. By 2020, that number had dropped to 1.51 billion square miles (3.92 billion sq km).

Polar bears depend on the ice cover for their survival. If it melts earlier and forms later, they go longer without food. Because of poor conditions, not as many cubs are born.

With more open water, orcas are swimming farther north. But they're not as familiar with that part of the Arctic. They may get trapped in sea ice when it freezes. Orcas can starve to death if this happens.

Worldwide efforts to stop or slow climate change must be supported. Otherwise, polar bears and orcas could become victims of climate change.

Workers in Russia help an
orca break free from ice.

POLAR BEAR

ORCA

Orcas are master ocean predators. Polar bears are the strongest and the biggest land carnivore. The orca knows how to stalk its prey. But the polar bear can smell prey from a distance.

Both of these Arctic predators are awesome. Which would be named the top predator? Is it the polar bear? Or is it the orca?

POLAR BEAR STATS

HEIGHT:
males: up to 10 feet (3 m)
females: up to 8 feet (2.4 m)

WEIGHT:
males: up to 1,700 pounds (771 kg)
females: up to 1,100 pounds (499 kg)

BIGGEST EVER RECORDED: 2,210 pounds (998 kg)

TYPES/SPECIES AROUND THE WORLD:
one species but 19 subpopulations

NUMBER OF TEETH: 42

PREY: ringed seals and bearded seals, walruses, beluga whales, small mammals, birds, eggs, vegetation

ORCA STATS

LENGTH: up to 33 feet (10 m)

WEIGHT: up to 22,000 pounds (9,979 kg)

BIGGEST EVER RECORDED: 32 feet (9.8 m) long and 22,050 pounds (10,001 kg)

NUMBER OF ECOTYPES AROUND THE WORLD: at least 10

NUMBER OF TEETH: 40–56

PREY: penguins, seals, fish, sea lions, dolphins, porpoises, sharks, rays, whales, octopi, squid, seabirds

GLOSSARY

adaptation (ad-uhp-TEY-shun)—a change in an animal that helps it survive better in a specific environment

biome (BYE-ohm)—a community of plants and animals in a major region of the planet

canine (KAY-nine)—a sharp tooth in the front part of the mouth

carnivore (KAHR-nuh-vohr)—an animal that eats only meat

consciousness (KON-shuhs-nis)—being fully aware of surroundings

echolocation (ek-oh-loh-KAY-shuhn)—locating objects using sound waves

ecosystem (EE-koh-sis-tuhm)—a group of animals and plants that work together with their surroundings

endurance (en-DUR-uhns)—the ability to keep doing an activity for long periods of time

evolve (i-VAHLV)—to change gradually over long periods of time

fluke (FLOOK)—a triangle-shaped part of an orca's tail

READ MORE

Marcos, Victoria. *Orcas*. Rosenberg, TX: Xist Publishing, 2019.

Rose, Rachel. *Orca*. New York: Bearport Publishing Company, 2020.

Stewart, David. *How Would You Survive as a Polar Bear?*
New York: Scholastic, 2021.

INTERNET SITES

National Geographic Kids: Killer Whale Facts!
natgeokids.com/uk/discover/animals/sea-life/killer-whale-facts/

National Geographic Kids: Ten Facts About the Arctic!
natgeokids.com/uk/discover/geography/general-geography/ten-facts-about-the-arctic/

World Wildlife Fund: Why do polar bears have white fur?
worldwildlife.org/stories/why-do-polar-bears-have-white-fur-and-nine-other-polar-bear-facts

INDEX

Arctic, 4, 5, 9, 26

biomes, 4

climate change, 13, 26

evolution, 5

orcas
  blubber, 4
  echolocation, 24
  endurance, 16
  hearing, 24
  hunting, 5, 12–13, 16,
    18–19, 24
  intelligence, 13
  other name for, 7
  pods, 13, 16, 19, 24
  prey, 6, 12, 16, 18, 19, 24,
    28, 29
  range, 5
  size, 29
  sleeping, 16
  speed, 5, 6, 18
  spyhopping, 24, 25
  stealth, 18–19, 28
  strength, 5, 12, 18
  teeth, 12, 29
  wave washing, 13, 16

polar bears
  claws, 9
  endurance, 14
  eyes, 9
  fat, 15
  fur, 9, 10
  hearing, 22
  hunting, 5, 9, 11, 14–15, 22
  paws, 4, 9
  prey, 8, 11, 14, 20–21, 28, 29
  range, 5
  scientific name, 23
  size, 10, 28, 29
  smelling, 20, 22, 28
  species, 29
  speed, 5, 8–9, 18
  stealth, 20–21
  strength, 5, 10–11, 18, 28
  swimming, 8, 14–15
  teeth, 11, 29